Life-size
Spiders
of Southern Ontario

Order: *Araneidae*

Printed in Canada

ISBN 0-9736272-4-7

FIN 05 01 07

Library and Archives Canada Cataloguing in Publication

Peters, Mike G., 1958-
    Life size spiders of southern Ontario / Mike G. Peters.

Includes index.
ISBN 978-0-9736272-4-4

    1. Spiders--Ontario, Southwestern--Identification. I. Title.

QL458.41.C2P47 2007   595.4'4097132   C2007-900223-4

Life-size
Spiders
of Southern Ontario

Order: *Araneidae*

Scale in Centimeters

N-S

Mike G. Peters
Life-size Macro Images since 1995

Foreword

The contents of this book are the result of weekly missions to seek out and photograph the unseen world that surrounds us, that we so often walk past without notice and scarcely know is here.

From the first thaws of spring, to the finality of fall, each Sunday afternoon {and sometimes Saturdays}, my friend and I would religiously devote at least three hours into searching through one of a number of different habitats, seeking the minuscule and camouflaged fragments of our local ecosystems. Covering an alternating variety of Microsystems through the span of each year, an overlap developed, whereby several of the area's forests, bogs, streams and marshes were given a thorough, seasonal coverage of their individualized flora and fauna - and the search goes on.

This book and others in my 'life-size' series, have been carefully put together by the composition of my broad collection into specially designed computer files, which are calibrated to maintain 'life-size' printed reproductions. These files were grouped by orders and families for quick reference and file locatability.

The style that I have chosen to portray my finds was not an easy one to choose. I felt it best to show as many variations as might be encountered and describe them sufficiently to give a sense that they live a life every day. I hope you enjoy the addition of blow-up enlargements as some of our spiders are very small.

Throughout my youth I was swamped with African, Australian and other nations creatures, with very little information about our own back yards. I hope that you will find my work sufficiently informative and awe-inspiring to appreciate the need for protection and respect toward the neighbourhoods that can't speak for themselves.

Preface

For much of my life I've been a point-n-shoot photographer during holidays and for special events - much like everyone else. During 1993 I began to tackle the subject with a totally different approach. I wanted to take photographs with sufficient clarity that I could draw my specimens - nothing more, or less.

Using a cheap focus-free camera and old binoculars that I had around the house, I could generate 12 and 16 power magnification; close range and distance shooting. I even built an extendable tripod [this was an improvement from a turn-seat chair base] with a plastic swivel/elevator mount. The biggest drawback was too much baggage and set-up time - I needed to make it one piece !

Using the binocular-lens to scrutinize my work one evening, it occurred to me to affix this very lens and test its field for focal distance and depth. Thus, during the late fall of 1994, scaled imagery had begun. I modified the camera face with cardboard to adapt a squared screw-mounting for the lens housing, to ensure a secure and flush mount. A wire gauge emanated to lay the span, centre-line and distance to field.

With the first wildlife footage came many observations of clarity, shading and the feel for the camera's versatility. Flash diffusion was the major immediate necessity to illuminate the under surfaces of my subjects without burning sunlit detail. I achieved this by engaging the camera-flash through various materials against a wall until I felt it soft enough, and perfected it slightly more through time. Not confined by a view-window to capture the alignment of my subjects, I am able to reach and manipulate an angle of observance from sometimes inhumanly obtuse perspectives [that is; my camera can infiltrate almost blindly where I can not get in and from angles I could never see].

The camera has evolved over time, mainly for look's sake and portability. The field is measured stem to stern and calibrated to a virtual 'life-sizing' by use of a pre-empted stage, compliant with a 'drafting scale', which both determined incremental measures of focus and, lens - camera / print-size configuration. The parameters of the focal field depict a number of balancings of counter-averaging to produce a very realistic and highly accurate, virtual life-size image of each individual subject - as viewed from the camera's angle of representation.

Although *Araneids* grow by moulting during the span of their lives, most of my specimens are relatively mature, and typical to those that you might encounter. Throughout the following pages, I have collaged together <u>169</u> life-size photographs and <u>159</u> enlargements of more than <u>48</u> different species into <u>76</u> spectacular colour pages.

The equipment I have created has altered my artistic hand, yet I must admit that following its lead has proven an unending realm of awe - and spiders are no exception.

I must surely give thanks to many for their promotion and enthusiasm through the preceding years and many more thanks to those who have taken active participation. Use of my father's computer, combined with his extras and odds-n-ends has been the ultimate in my collection's refinement; yet without participation and help from my deceased friend and colleague Albert VanOmmen, the challenges may have been too far to travel. Since the passing of my friend Albert, I have devoted my life into the creation of these fine books, of which he had placed so much of his genuine faith.

Please enjoy the following pages that I have selected and generated to be seen and enjoyed by all.

<u>Note</u>: Complimentary with life-size pictures in this book are enlargements marked '**#.0x**'

Acknowledgements

This photography has drawn excitement from its beginnings, but without prodding and enthusiastic drive by individuals close to me, I would have set it aside a long while back. The trials and tribulations have been many and varied – and increase as I modify my means and measures to suit an ever expanding result.

I have been to many photo-lab processors during the initial years, but John Jamieson stands out for calibrating his equipment to suit my work, until I could calibrate mine to suit his; although a young lady named Jamie was the first, upon realizing the gist of my work. To the rest of the processors over time – I thank you all for your gracious conduct and professionalism. My methods and equipment are now through digitized methods.

To my parents and family who have given their all in support of my space {among many other helpful deeds}, I have at least brought the wonders of nature into our homes. I must also thank my long-time neighbour Isabel Lawrence, for proofreading this book for my typos and errors.

To my friends and others who have come on odd hikes, I hope to do it more often, and to all who appreciate the work that I do, I'll continue describing the subtle world around us. I also must give appreciation to the University of Guelph for the lengthy loan of reference books.

To the good people at the Stone Road Mall, Chapters Book Store and Steven Lewis, {on behalf of the Guelph Public Library}, for their eagerness and appreciation of holding my displays, I thank you for your initial interests in the value of my works, and hope that they attracted at least a few good souls.

Sadly, on May 18, 2002, my close friend and comrade of 17 years, 'Albert Henk VanOmmen' passed his life to the elements in an accident of fate while we were on our usual spring holiday 'assignment'. He was instrumental in more than just the evolution of this photography, but a devoted assistant in any challenge presented. He was as solid and reliable a man as one might ever encounter - easy going, open minded and always ready to help – a true friend to be proud of. Of all the people who may peruse through my books, I'd always expected he would see them not only first, but in every phase besides. To Albert I devote my greatest thanks and ultimate appreciation.

I sincerely hope that you enjoy this book on behalf of all through time who have supplied the energies and paths which brought such realism before you in present.

Sincerely,
Mike G. Peters
innovator/photographer
Life-size Macro Images since 1995

Introduction

Spiders are ancient creatures that came into being both before the Carboniferous period and vertebrates, yet due to the fragility of their delicate bodies, fossil records do not go back in time sufficiently to establish the full roots of their diverse evolution. They have since established a niche in almost every terrestrial habitat from mountain peaks and caves, marshes and deserts, to the nooks and crannies around your home. Some are hunters and others are web-spinners, while others can walk on water - and others again can even swim.

Spiders hatch as miniature {sexually undeveloped} replicas of their more colourful adults and bear from a single, simple eye {found in some deep cave dwellers} to two, four, six, or eight, depending on their use of vision. The spiderlings quickly disperse and emit long lengths of fine silk into the breeze, called gossamer, which eventually counters their slight of mass and they are airborne to balloon away - drifting abroad from a few metres to hundreds of kilometres and raised aloft in the breeze often to thousands of metres into the atmosphere!

Araneids have eight legs and possess the ability to regenerate a lost appendage over a period of about three moults, which typically number from four to ten in some larger species and is determined greatly by spider size. They have fangs folded below their chclicerae to seize and envenomate their prey, below their eyes in fore of their face. A tough casing surrounds their carapace and legs while their abdomens are mainly soft and fleshy, containing the heart, lungs, intestines, female reproductive organs, silk glands and spinnerets.

Spiders are friendly creatures that feed on the multitudes of truly unwanted insects invading our yards such as earwigs, ants, flies and dozens of serious garden pests. Although they might be venomous, spiders will not bite you if you do not disturb their precious world.

Contents

Spiders

Jumping Spiders
Salticidae

Savannah Jumper
Evarcha hoyi

3.5x

Female jumping spiders, such as the one shown above, are typically larger than their male counterparts and may be easily recognised by their smaller forelegs and closer posture.

These medium sized jumping spiders are usually found running and jumping about in tall grass, on shrubs and trees around forest edges near streams and rivers from New England {including Southern Ontario} to Pennsylvania, and westward across to the Pacific coast.

Evarcha hoyi females grow from 4.6-6.3mm with males from 4.3-5.5mm. Females overwinter and live for more than twelve months.

Salticids are wandering hunting spiders that build a small silken retreat to rest, escape bad weather and to lay their eggs. They use a silken dragline to secure themselves from falling, both when moving about and leaping outward to capture prey. They do not build webs.

Woodland Jumper
Habrocestum pulex

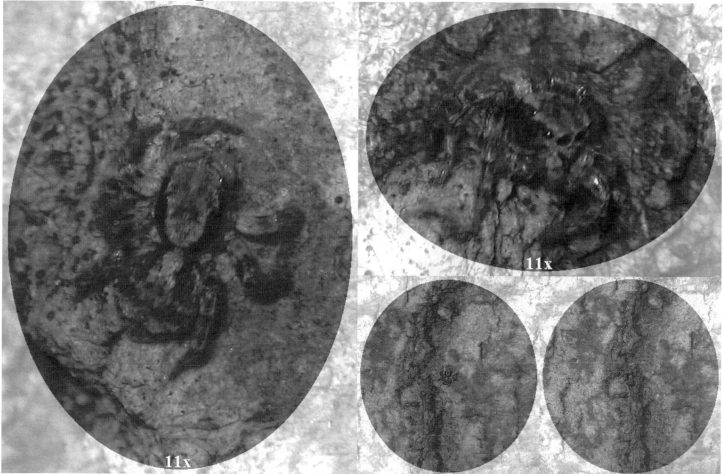

Easily seen in the enlarged pictures, the life-size images along the lower right show these spiders blend in perfectly with their surroundings. These jumpers are common on trees.

You may well encounter these small jumpers on tree trunks, their branches or on the forest floor in among the ample mosses and fallen debris. They are quite common in wooded areas east of the Rockies.

H. pulex are small jumpers with both sexes growing to about 5mm. Although the markings are very similar with those of *S. palustris*, these prefer the open woods, taking advantage of their camouflage.

The diet of these spiders would likely consist of flies, small beetles, aphids, butterflies and other insects common to their habitat, although they are just as likely to tackle small spiders, straying in their path.

These small jumpers will overwinter and live at least twelve months.

Common Wall Jumper
Sitticus palustris

5.4x

9.9x

Having a particular liking for man and his world, these harmless and friendly little jumpers may be seen on your brickwork and siding, on your garden plants, hopping across your patio furniture and may even pop into your home from time to time. The males are smaller on average, and are generally darker than the females.

These are the most common and abundant little spiders that inhabit the multitudes of internal crevaces and man made passages within the outer walls of our homes and structures in our gardens. They are very well known domestically from New England to the Pacific Coast.

S. palustris are not only incapable of biting because of the small size and positioning of their fangs, but these jumpers can be quite friendly.

The lighter females grow from 5-6mm and males from 3.5-5mm. The young begin to appear in June and adults phase away in July, lending a longevity of thirteen to fourteen months. The adolescent spiders group together to hibernate in safe, unexposed places through winter.

9.6x

9.5x

9x

Jumping spiders have the sharpest and keenest vision of all spiders. The top, right enlargement of a young female shows the main large saucer eyes facing foreward on her carapace with a smaller pair shouldered behind them, and the top left view depicts another pair shouldered about half-way back, with a tiny indistinguishable pair midway.

These household jumpers prey on pesky moths, flies and little bugs.

Zebra Jumper
Salticus scenicus

A male is depicted in the upper left corner, with the rest being views of a female. The females have light chevrons atop the abdomens and a light wishbone mark on the carapace, which are absent on the males. Notice the penetrating eyes in the lower left view.

These well known jumpers occur naturally among rocks, yet are abundant on the outer walls of buildings and pransing along fences. They commonly inhabit most of North America and much of Europe.

The females grow from 4.3-6.4mm and males from 4-5.5mm.

S. scenicus live about one year and although they often stray indoors, they are friendly and harmless creatures, preying on unwelcome pests.

Bankside Jumper
Metaphidippus protervus

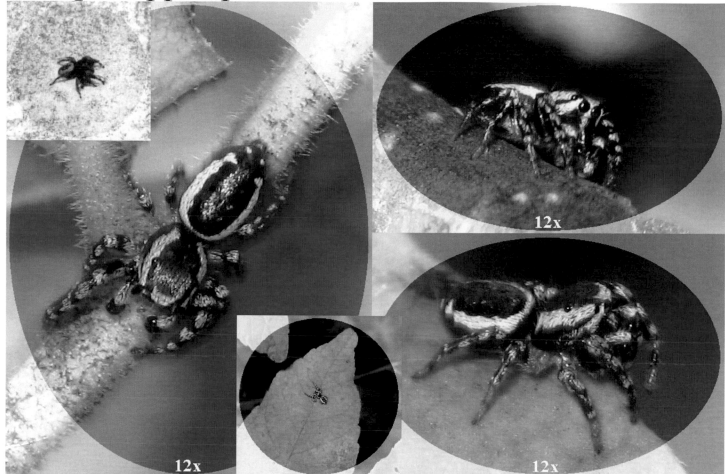

Typical to jumpers, the juvenile male at bottom/centre (and enlarged views) moved in short, precise bursts, swaying from side to side to gain the best view of its surroundings. A mature female is shown at the top/left. These spiders are very common around lakes and rivers and you'll often notice them on structures with plain coloured surfaces.

These mid-sized predators are abundant in meadows and in woods on foliage, fence posts and in tall grasses near sources of water. They are found east of the Rockies and are more common north than south.

Ranging from a lesser 3-4.4mm in males to a considerable 3.7-6.3mm in females, these spiders run freely and set an anchor line only when leaping on prey. They have powerful chelicerae and can bite.

The female constructs a cocoon for her eggs attached to twigs and remains close by. Once hatched the spiderlings disperse rapidly.

Common among jumpers, these are sun-loving, daytime hunters.

Decorated Jumper
Habronattus decorus

12x

12x

9.6x

9.6x

These jumpers, like sveral others have adhesive scopulae on their feet, giving them the ability to walk on smooth surfaces, including the sheer face of glass. Notice the fiery gleam of the male along the bottom and the fore-eyes of the darker-bodied female above. These contrasting spiders may be found around the walls of our homes and in our gardens.

  H. decorus are common around homes and gardens in the southern regions of our area, and into the central, eastern United States.
  The females may be yellow to brown with light markings separated by dark, and grow to 5-6mm, while the more brilliant males grow from 4-5mm. They overwinter in sheltered crevices about half grown.

Meadow Jumper
Phidippus clarus rimator

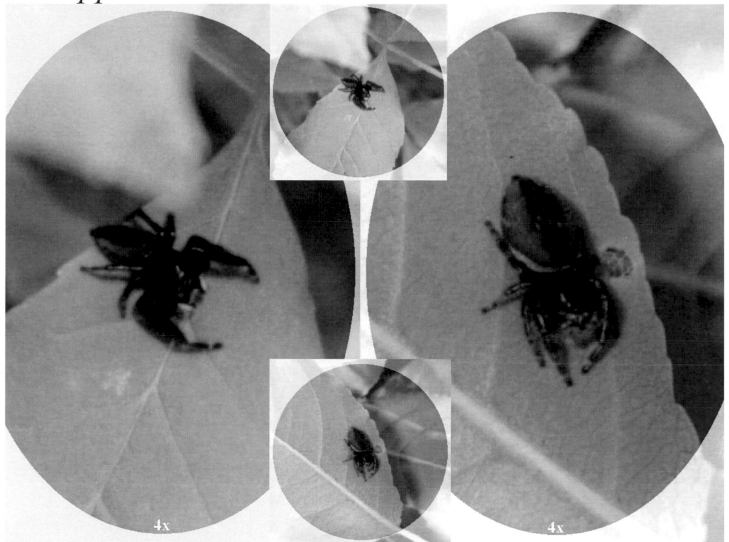

The stockier male is visualized at left and top centre, with the larger and more brilliant female at right and bottom centre. These relatively large spiders would prefer to remain out of sight, yet are capable of biting, and are known to have medium strength venom.

This medium sized species is the most common of the *Phidippus* genus, thriving in the tall grasses and bushes of our open meadows. They are widely distributed and abundant throughout North America.

These jumpers are known for their magnificent leaps when pouncing on prey and are excellent hunters. *Phidippus* can tackle damselflies, butterflies and moths, and their fast acting poison allows the capture of livelier crickets, grasshoppers and katydids, with very little struggle.

Daring Jumper
Phidippus audax

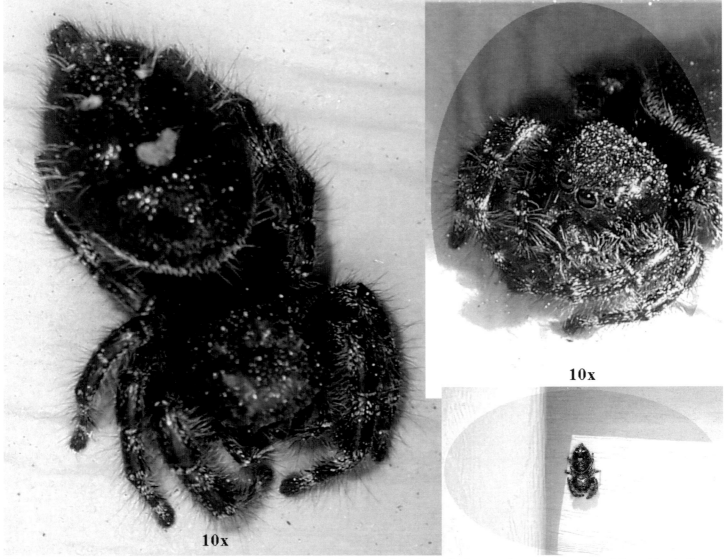

10x

10x

The cute little puppy-dog eyes of this female can be deceiving when you consider that they belong to our largest and most venomous local jumping spider. I met this little darling in the same location at two separate times, and she could spot me from ten feet away. Having previously built her trust, I was able to coax her into the open to take these photographs.

Daring Jumpers are common under stones and boards and may be seen running over tree trunks in woods and around your garden. They are found from the Atlantic coast to the Rocky Mountains, throughout the United States and into southern Canada. They commonly enter our homes, hunting on windowsills and sachets for insects to feast on.

The females may live for eighteen months and range from 10-15mm

3.7x

3.7x

7.5x

The spectacular male shown above was brought to me by a friend who found it bounding around in their home. Notice the fangs in the lower left frame, capable of a painful bite.

and the males a formidable 6-13mm. The male courts a female by wavering his forelegs in a species unique but typical *Salticid* style. The female attends her egg sac until the spiderlings safely disperse.

Bridge Jumper
Metacyrba undata

10x

3x

The top left and enlarged lower right inlays show this spider's face, while in the central view, he's tilting his head back to vividly show its large brown eyes above a lower brow of orange hairs, and a tuft of white whiskers moustache above his chelicerae.

These bold jumpers may be found sheltering under bark, but are usually found skipping over fences and along stone walls. They are common throughout the eastern United States to Wisconsin and Texas. The females grow from 10-13mm and males from 8.5-9.5mm. Like many jumpers, *M. undata* may leap forty times their own body length and can tackle damselflies, butterflies and moths. Their fast acting poison allows the capture of feisty crickets, grasshoppers and katydids.

Bridge Jumper

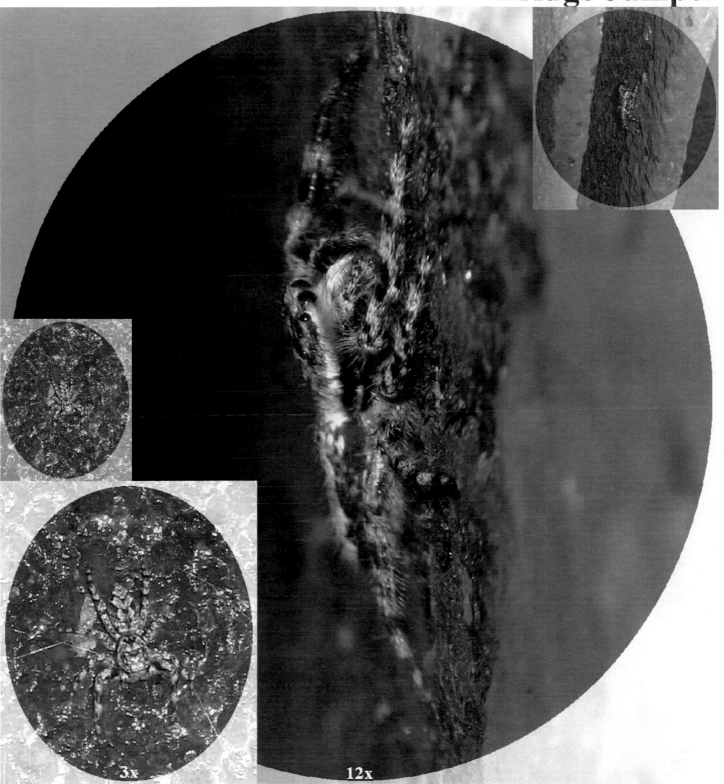

3.x

12x

The stealth, camoflauge and strength of these spiders allow them to rule in their chosen domain. Popping in and out from between the girders of a bridge, this jumper proved quite difficult to photograph. Although not notably venomous, this spider can and will bite. *M. undata* prefer high open positions to leap outward at flying damselflies and such. These spiders have a longevity of about eighteen months, thriving for two full seasons.

Crab Spiders
Philodromidae and Thomisidae

Travelling Crab Spider
Xysticus transversatus ferox

10x

The sexes in this species are often dimorphic and hard to distinguish in immature subjects. These crab spiders are always on the move in search of unsuspecting hoverflies, flies and even large butterflies, but are always alert to avoid spider-hunting wasps.

You may notice these creatures creeping along the wall of your home, under bark and debris in the forest, or on foliage in meadows, from Newfoundland to Alberta and south to New Mexico and Georgia. The females may be 6-7mm and the darker males from 5-6mm. These spiders are daytime hunters, walking either fore or sideways.

Elegant Crab Spider
Xysticus elegans

9.2x

4.6x

Shown at top/right is a tiny spiderling, a juvenile at left and adults across the bottom. Crab spiders extend their strong front legs and snap shut to catch their prey, implanting their small fangs into the neck and allowing the strong nerve venom to calm their victim.

These medium/large crab-like spiders stalk their prey on small shrubs and flowering plants, often waiting in ambush at likely spots. They are common from New England to the Rockies and south to Georgia.

Flower Spider
Misumena vatia

10x

2.9x

3x

When you spot a fly, butterfly or other flower-visiting insect that doesn't seem quite right, there's probably a crab spider holding fast to its head. Flower spiders wait patiently on flowers for their prey to come to them, often changing colours slightly to remain unseen.

These flower dwelling spiders live entirely on plants and flowers in virtually every meadow and clearing throughout most of the continent.
The females range from 6-9mm and males from 2.9-4mm. The eggs are laid in folded silk-sealed leaves on shrubs in mid-summer and they overwinter half grown. Their eight tiny eyes provide very near vision.

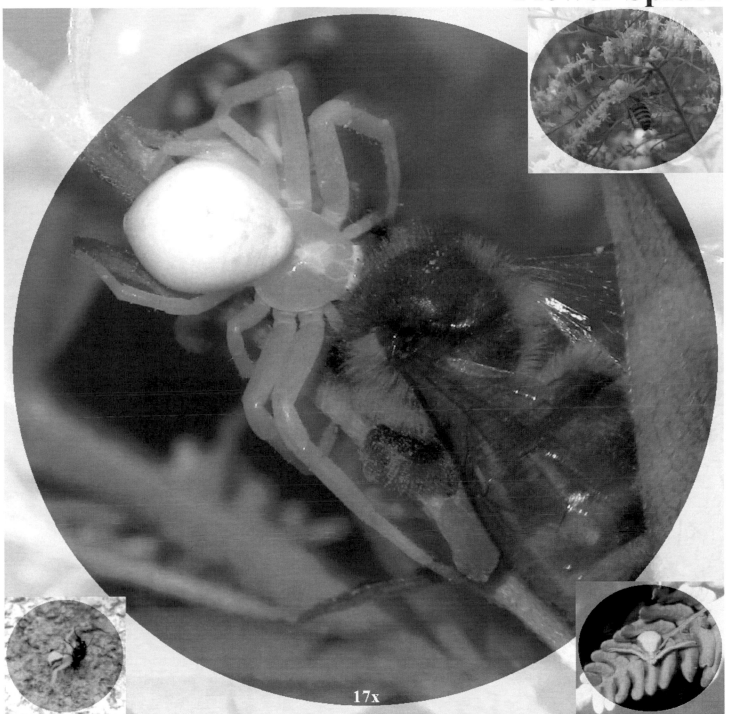

17x

Flower spiders are usually yellow or white and may or may not have red stripes on their abdomens. All crab spiders have very small eyes and poor vision, relying on pheromones to help attract their prey, and vibrations to know when it is near enough to see.

With superb camouflage and physical design, *M. vatia* are very adept at capturing stinging insects such as flying ants and bees, yet they also enjoy butterflies and moths. Their small fangs hold fast, potent venom.

Large Flower Spider
Misumenoides formosipes aleatorius

3.8x

14.3x

These beautiful crab spiders are very similar to the previous *M. vatia*, yet their markings enter onto the central abdomen, and the females grow slightly larger. I believe that it is a young male shown in the lower right, having taken colouration from the aster it is on.

These flower spiders are found in similar habitats as the previous *M. vatia*, in meadows, fields and gardens on flowers, yet their range is more restricted to the warmer United States and southern Canada.

The females may be from 5-11.3mm and males from a meager 2.5-3.2mm. Like others in kind they feed on flower-visiting insects and are a necessary natural population control on oftentimes nuisance pests.

Bristly Crab Spider
Misumenops asperatus

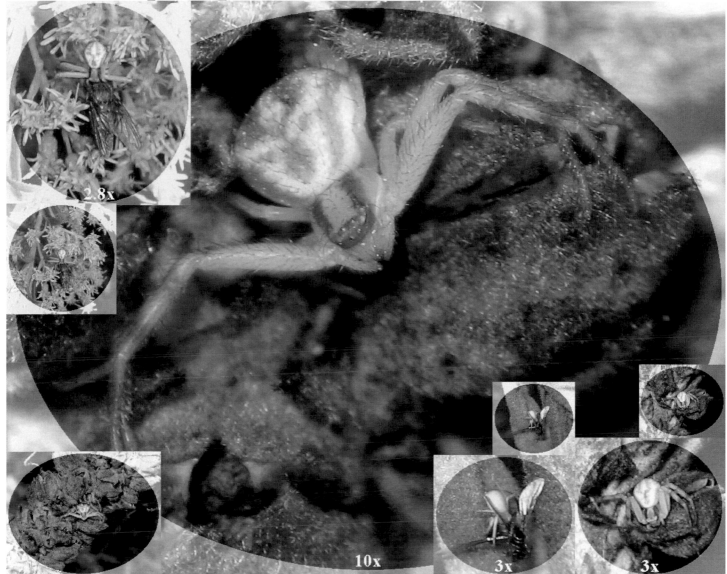

All of the spiders above were collected in the fall and will overwinter to breed in the late spring. Most of these spiders were found in mullein seed spikes, although they also prey among foliage in shrubs and trees. Look carefully at the very tiny eyes and the fine bristly hairs covering most of their bodies and legs, unlike their smoother *Misumen* cousins.

These hairy spiders are found throughout the eastern United States as far southwest as Utah. They prey on ants, bees and flies in open grassy areas, amid the flowers and foliage of adjacent trees and shrubs.

The females grow from 4.4-6mm in length, with males being 3-4mm. These annual spiders are heavily culled by dauber wasps and birds.

Spotted Grass Spider
Tibellus oblongus

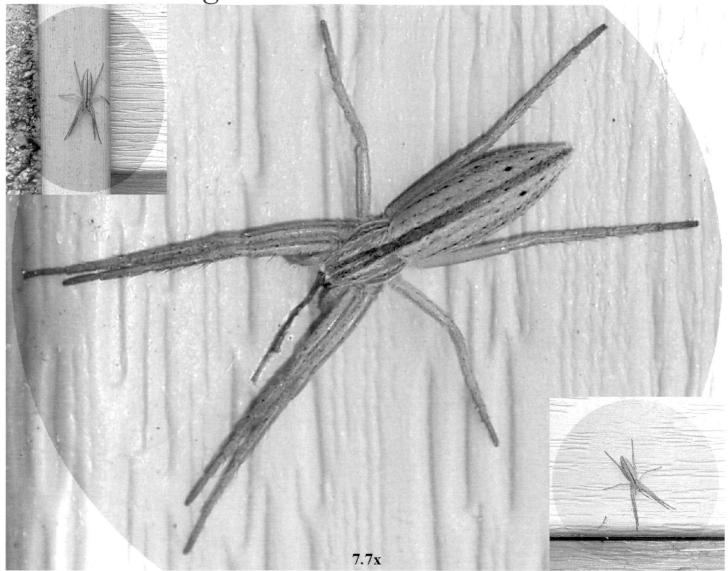

7.7x

These long-bodied crab spiders resemble *T. duttoni**, yet are differentiated by the paired black spots near the end of the abdomen. Although normally found on the blades of high grass, this one found the siding of my home a suitable place for shelter and good hunting.

Normally found in bushes and tall grass, these slim bodied spiders can run rapidly, and can fling outward to catch flying insects, even eating larger spiders. Both *T. oblongus* and *T. duttoni* are common in most of southern Canada, and throughout the United States.

The females grow from 7-9mm and the males from 6-8mm. They are light gray or yellow with darker dorsal stripes along their length.

Ground Spiders
Gnaphosidae

Black Ground Spider
Gnaphosa muscorum

8.5x

G. muscorum are medium/large spiders hunting mainly at night from their tubular silken retreats made under flat laid objects in pastures, wooded areas and in gardens.

These ground spiders are common from New England to Arizona and across to the Pacific Coast. There are several species in our area.

Domestic Hunting Spiders
Clubionidae

Slender Sac Spider
Chiracanthium mildei

7x

10x

Fortunately we have no deadly poisonous spiders in our area, yet you probably won't appreciate having this one around your home. These spiders are notably painful biters with medium strength venom that can cause acute to severe systematic reactions during the first day, followed by mild necrosis which persists over the next few days.

These nocturnal hunters are rare in the wild, yet have become the most dominant house spider in their class. Presumed to have been introduced circa 1950 from Europe, they are now established in Japan and both Americas - central/eastern America where we are concerned.
The females are typically from 7-10mm and males from 5.8-8.5mm with more slender bodies and longer legs. These spiders hunt from their retreat, which is spun into an oval cell of tightly woven silk, made under stones, plant-pots and in crevices of buildings, often

Slender Sac Spider

6.9x

3.7x

3.8x

From cream and yellow to red or green, you may discover *C. mildei* in colours due to their previous meal, which ranges from moths to craneflies and various other pests. These eerie looking spiders are very clumsy, slow moving and short-sighted, six-eyed hunters.

entering our homes in search of warm, dark, humid surroundings. Slender Sac spiders may be encountered year round, preferring to live outside during the warmer months and moving back in during fall.

Wolf Spiders
Lycosidae

Thin-legged Wolf Spider
Pardosa spp.

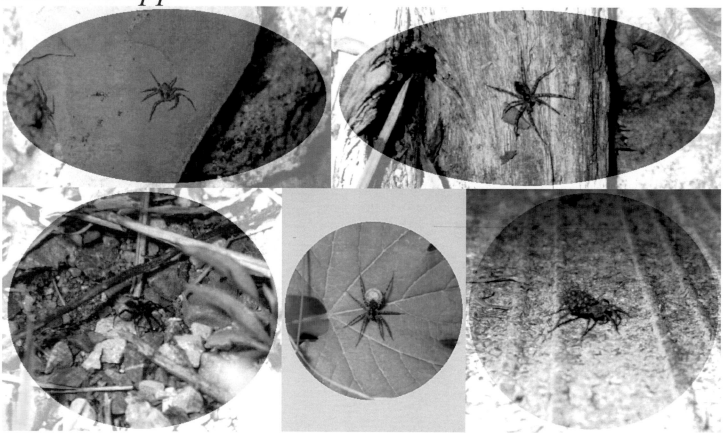

There are several species of these small, sun-loving wolf spiders in our area, which may live more than a year in the extreme north. At bottom left and centre are females carrying their egg sacs, and a mother carrying her young on her back at the lower right. The spiderlings balloon in summer and pre-adults trail gossamer across roadways in fall.

These large eyed vagrant spiders do not build retreats and may be found in woods on wet ground, or in open grassy fields, while some prefer stony shorelines and clay banks. Most local species range from New England to the Rockies, south to Arizona and North Carolina.

The females range from 4.5-9.5mm and the males from 4-7mm. The males perform a species specific dance with their forearms to entice

Thin-legged Wolf Spider

6x

4x

4x

These keen-eyed hunters have the ability to run across water and are very successful at culling a number of large and small insects. These welcome creatures were in my yard.

the female into courtship, in a similar fashion with the jumpers. The male palps are keyed to the female epigyne, annulling interbreeding.

Common Wolf Spider
Lycosa avida

These wandering wolf spiders have variable markings and were found in my front garden within a day or so of each other. Most other wolf spiders have a dark heart patch at the fore portion of their abdomens. Movement triggers the pursuit of prey, and wolf spiders as a group are mildly venomous, with powerful chelicerae.

These spiders may be found roaming in fields and gardens or among leaf litter in woodlands and forests throughout North America.

With a longevity of about eighteen months, these females may grow from 10-15mm and the males {albeit shorter lived} from 8-11mm.

Tunnelling Wolf Spider
Lycosa helluo

3.7x

These are the largest wolf spiders that I have found in our area. A female is shown at top left and her male suitor below her. A female guards her egg sac under a stone at the right.

Found in the United States and southern Canada, these rather large spiders inhabit open fields on the ground, feeding on various insects.

Nursery Web Spiders
Pisauridae

Silver-bordered Fishing Spider
Dolomedes scriptus

The young males shown above are about a year old and will live throughout the next summer season as well. These spiders have been seen dabbling their fore feet into the water at the edge of a lily pad, tantalizing small fish in the fashion of a fisherman's lure.

These stealthy spiders grow to be quite large and are common near rivers and in adjacent woods. They may often be seen walking on the water's surface from New England to Florida and west to the Rockies.

The females grow from a formidable 17-24mm and males from 13-16mm. They feed on large shoreline insects, tadpoles and small fish.

These sharp-eyed hunters can't swim, but can crawl below the water

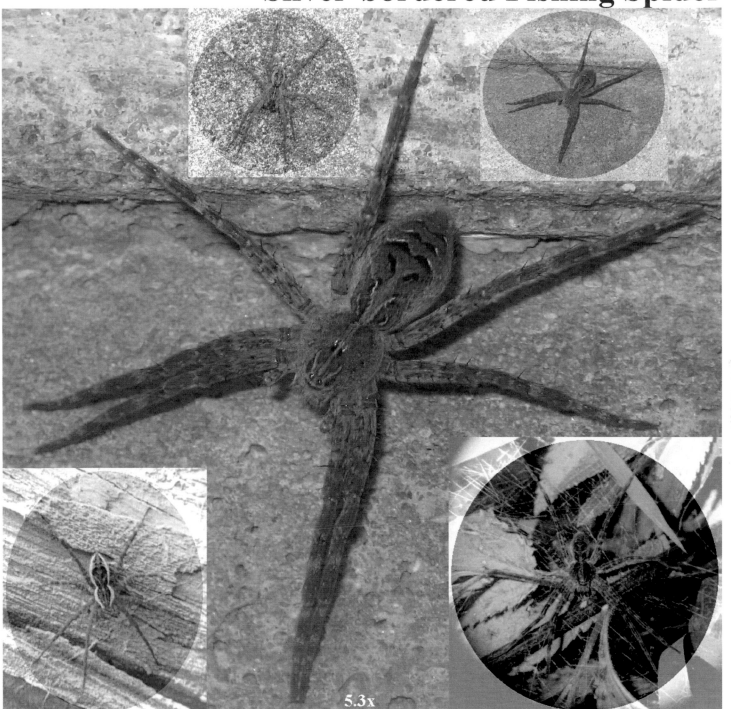

5.3x

These spiders can grow large and not only would a bite from their fangs be painful, but I've had the potency of their venom equated with a serious bout of influenza. The nursery webs may be over a foot long and as much as eight inches in diameter.

to hunt, where they may remain for up to thirty minutes.

The females carry egg-sacs containing about 300 eggs for two to three weeks, often laying several batches during a single season.

Dock Spider
Dolomedes tenebrosus

These are the largest spiders in our area and are very similar to the previously described *D. scriptus* in appearances, habitats, capabilities and life cycles. The major differences are that *D. tenebrosus* are darker, lack light 'W' chevrons on the abdomen and are larger.

Although usually seen near water, dock spiders are often found some distance away in adjacent wooded areas. They are numerous near rivers from New England to Florida and west to the Rockies.

The females range from 15-26mm and the males from 7-13mm. They use their strong legs and potent venom to prey on larger insects, small fish and amphibians etc, and may well take small rodents as well.

The female attaches her egg sac at the top of a herb, then builds a nursery enclosed in leaves, guarding outside until spiderlings depart.

Fisher Spider
Dolomedes triton

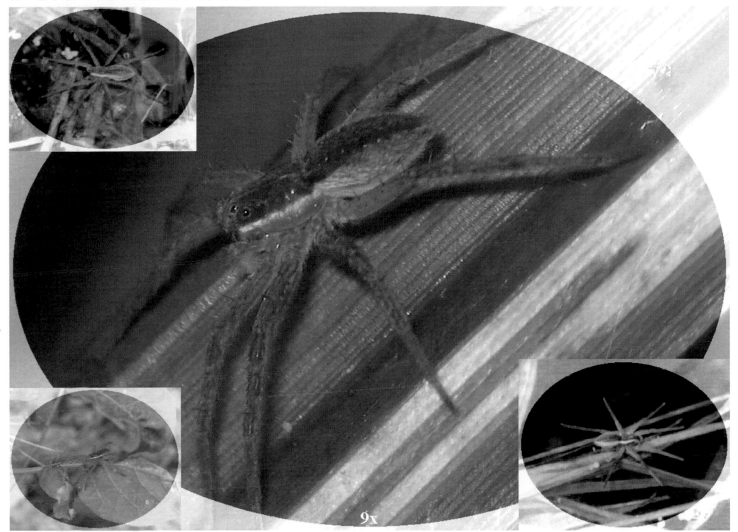

These are the only truly aquatic spiders in the *Dolomedes* family, and they can close their tibial hairs, releasing the air cushion below their feet, allowing them to sink below the water, and they simply swim down to the bottom weed-beds. The light spots along the sides of the abdomen are often pronounced in older, mature specimens.

Although most *Dolomedes* prefer the ebbs and pools of flowing water, I typically encounter these among the bullrushes and well vegetated still waters of shallow ponds and bogs. *D. triton* are common throughout the United States, east of the Rocky Mountains.
The males are typically 10mm and the females grow up to a sizable 20mm. Like most other nursery-web spiders, Fisher Spiders have a longevity of about two seasons, overwintering among the rushes.

Nursery Web Spider
Pisaurina mira

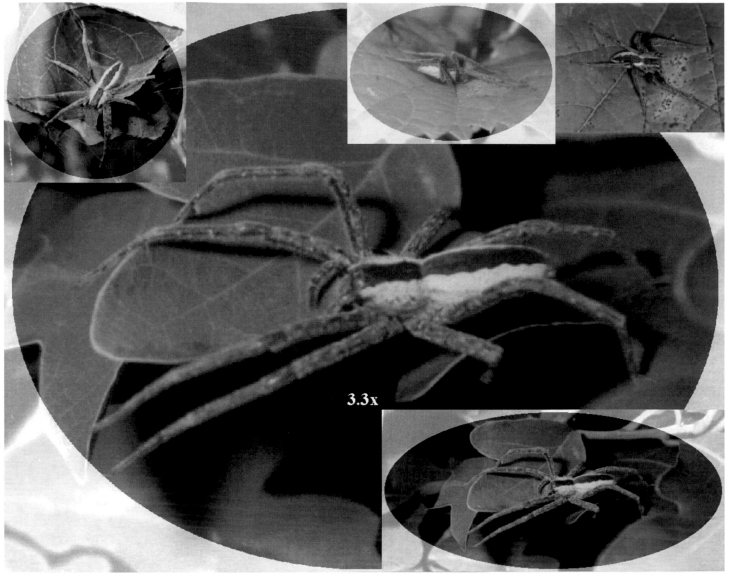

3.3x

As with their sister *Dolomedes* and cousin *Lycosas'*, these Nursery Web Spiders are sharp-eyed predators and only use silk in the construction of their nurseries. Unlike typical *Dolomedes*, *P. mira* are non-amphibious, often being found quite a distance from water.

Pisaurina mira are relatively common in the southern portions of our region, living on bushes, low vegetation and grasses, in woods and meadows from New England to Nebraska, south to Florida and Texas.
The females range from 12.5-16.5mm and males from 10.5-15mm. They are wandering hunters, preying on an assortment of unsuspecting small and large insects, including damselflies and dragonflies.

3.8x

Carrying their egg sacs through June and July, female nursery-webs build their nurseries in advance in shrubs and weeds, and guard them until the spiderlings disperse in the fall.

Sheet-web Weavers
Agelenidae

Grass Funnel-weaver
Agelena labyrinthica

3x

The more available food, the bigger a spider will grow, and the allure of the porch light at my home draws a never ending abundance to line their webs around my door, which is not the case for the one shown at the bottom, right, since he misses the night-life action.

The funnel-shaped retreat and horizontal sheet are common sights in grassy areas, in woods among low shrubs, on stone fences and around our homes. They are known across most of central North America.

The females grow from 10-17mm and the males from 9-13mm. The

5.9x

The lower right view shows a male courting the larger female by cautiously tapping on threads of her web. Although both are very fast, the male's superior agility allows him to seize the female, bringing her into her retreat to mate. The convex egg sacs are laid in fall.

funnel-weavers are best recognised by their exposed sheet web tucked into corners and rock-piles. The funnel-shaped retreat is a deep labyrinth extending into a crevice or attached leaves, is open at both ends, and is built by accretion throughout their one season life-span.

Funnel-weavers rely on hopping and hapless insects to bounce on their sheet and sink, alerting the spider, which darts out and dashes to envenomate its prey upright, dragging it into its retreat to feast. They may bite big insects several times, withdrawing from the larger ones.

Common House Spider
Tegenaria domestica

10x

These funnel-weavers live inside your home in the corners of your basement, behind the washing machine and the like. A youngster is shown at the top, left and enlargement, with middle-aged females kiddie-corner from top, right. Often moving outdoors in summer and returning to the warmth of our homes in fall, these spiders may live for several years.

Living under stones and rocks, in caves, hollow trees, crevices in barns and cellars, room corners and wall openings, *T. domestica* build their small funnel-shaped webs in dark corners. They are cosmopolitan spiders, introduced to become widespread throughout North America.

The females grow to be between 7.5-11.5mm, and the hefty males from 6-9mm. You may encounter mature spiders at any time of year, and in any season. They have large fangs and are known to be mildly venomous, biting humans if disturbed, and may live for several years.

Unusual in spiders, male house spiders live with the females for two to three months during the breeding season, and are often encountered

5.4x

2.4x

Growing rather large, adult males like this one prowling around your home are the number one source of arachnophobia - worldwide. Notice the intricate and large palps, with a sperm packet readied, as is apparent in the top lateral view enlargement.

wandering through your home in search of females, with the males outstanding pedipalps giving rise to arachnophobia.

Six-eyed Spiders
Pholcidae

Long-bodied Cellar Spider
Pholcus phalangioides

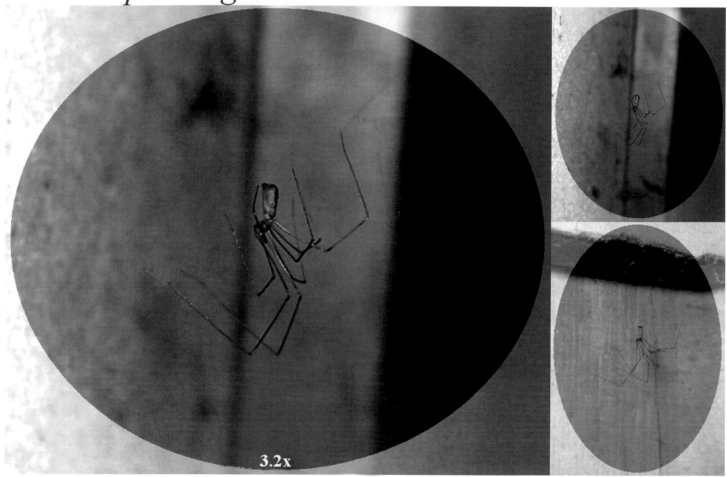

3.2x

These are the 'daddy-long-legs' that live inside your home; and the species name *P. phalangioides* refers to the order of the same-name harvestmen relatives, which live outside your home, and are not spiders at all. You may find these spiders in the corners of rooms, behind large appliances, and especially in the rafters of your basement.

P. phalangioides are the most common household spiders in temperate North America. Their irregular webs are common in cellars and dark, quiet locations throughout your home. They hang inverted, and large females may be found holding an egg sac in their chelicerae.

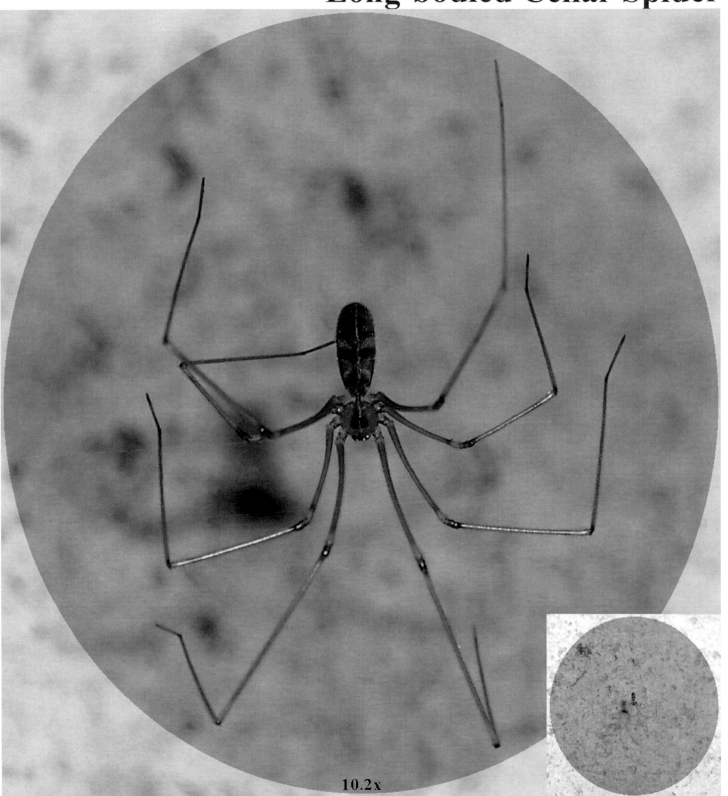

10.2x

This is the same small representative as seen on the previous page. Older mature females are more yellow in body colour and grow to a sizable 8mm, with males to 6mm. Females are common all year, and may live for several, with males seen from spring to fall. These spiders will vibrate intensely if disturbed, blurring away in the darkness.

Comb-footed Spiders
Theridiidae

False Widow Spider
Steatoda borealis

18x

18x

The tiny male above has hefty chelicerae, resembling suction-cups from their bottom view. *S. borealis* are common in the wild, yet the same is true around our homes and gardens.

These dark spiders are common in the northern states and Canada.

11.8x

11.8x

This mature female built her meshed web between my shovel and a rake, taking refuge under the shovel's foot-curl. These are mildly venomous spiders, preferring red ants, woodlice, small beetles and flies to suffice their diet. They typically hide by day.

Red and White Spider
Enoplognatha ovata redimitum

7.1x

3.8x

The males of this species (right) have enormous, powerful chelicerae and long fangs. Their potent venom is effective against prey as large as bumble bees, and being common spiders around our homes, they often bite unsuspecting gardeners with reportable, nasty bites.

These are common from the north-eastern Maritimes to the Pacific.

Red and White Spider

The female above guarded her egg sac until the spiderlings hatched, and lived into the early fall. *E. redimitum* fling sticky threads over bees and beetles and such, repeatedly envenomating their prey several times, and then wrapping them with more silk.

Domestic House Spider
Achaearanea tepidariorum

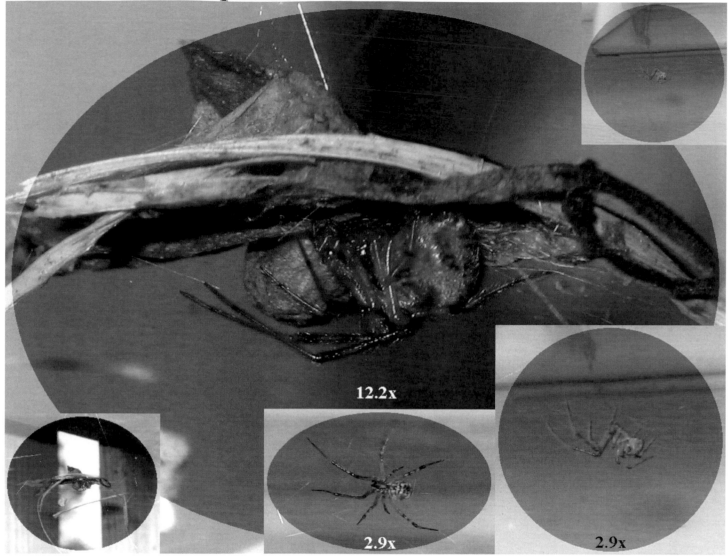

12.2x

2.9x

2.9x

These spiders have often been recorded for the intrinsic strength of their large snares, known to subdue snakes and mice, and able to kill them with their potent venom - yet they seem to be content feeding on ants, carwigs and other nuisance insects around the yard.

These introduced spiders to North America are extremely common in and outside of homes, barns, in corners of windows, doorframes, between fence boards, under stones, around bridges and in the forests. The females are typically 5-6mm and males from 3.8-4.7mm. The adults are found in all seasons, and may live more than a year once they are mature. Although they may be found in a range of colours, the legs of males are orange, and the females are lighter with dark bands.

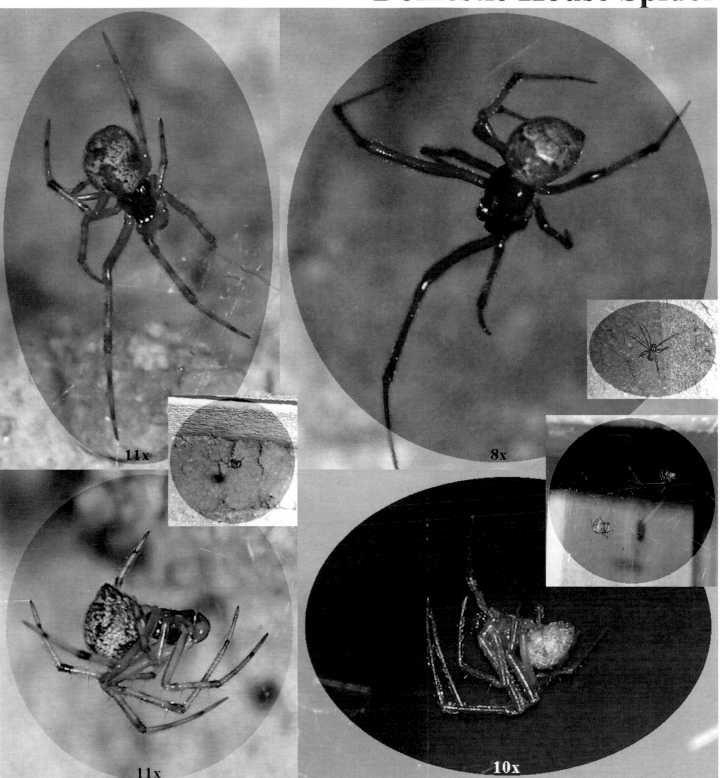

11x

8x

11x

10x

The male at lower right is courting a female. A female is depicted along the left. The females make brownish, ovoid to pear-shaped egg sacs in tough papery covers, usually hanging them openly in their web. *A. tepidariorum* sit open in their webs, collecting debris and small leaves from the breeze for shelter. You might also notice old prey left dangling in their webs, adding carcasses to hide amid against the ever prowling spider wasps.

Corner Spiders
Achaearanea rupicola

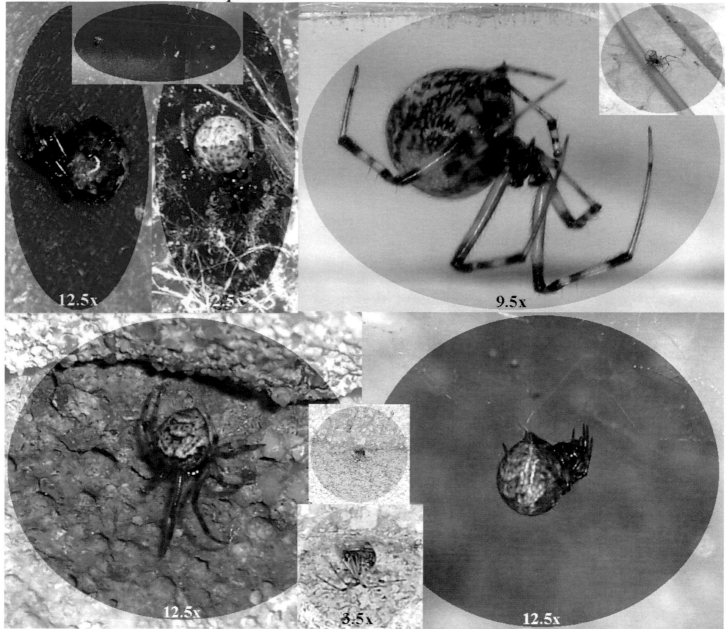

When you move something from a corner on your patio with debris littered cobwebs fixed on, you may notice what appears to be a number of tiny grains dropping to the ground, like particles of sand. These communal spiders are extremely common around the home.

These are common spiders, dwelling under stones and boards in woods, and are also at home around houses. They are known from New England to Alabama and westward across to the Mississippi.

A. rupicola typically feed on mosquitoes, ants, woodlice, etc.

Line Weavers
Linyphiidae

Filmy Dome Weaver
Prolinyphia marginata

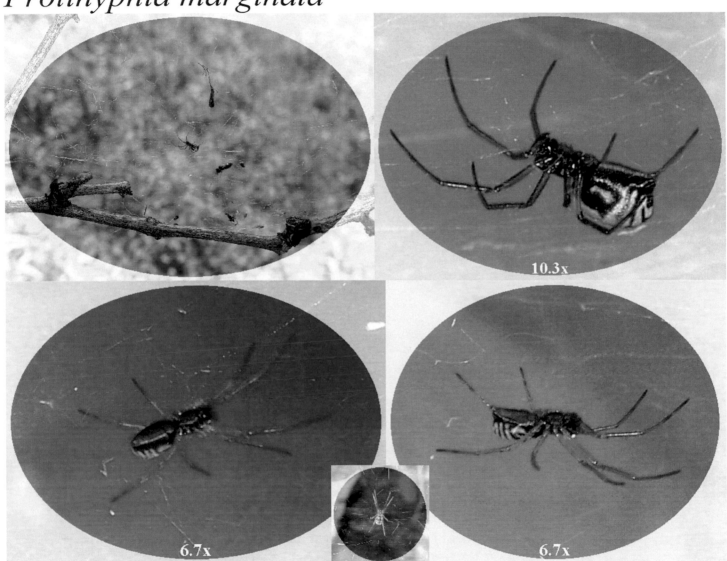

The characteristic and very common roundish, domed snares of these spiders are abundant, and very efficient in trapping clumsy insects, such as hoppers and the sort. The effectiveness of their webs have made them one of the most prolific of all araneids.

P. marginata prefer moist wooded areas and weedy clearings, in rock piles, stone walls, weeds and trees, both in North America and Europe.

Venomless Spiders
Uloboridae

Feather-legged Spider
Uloborus glomosus

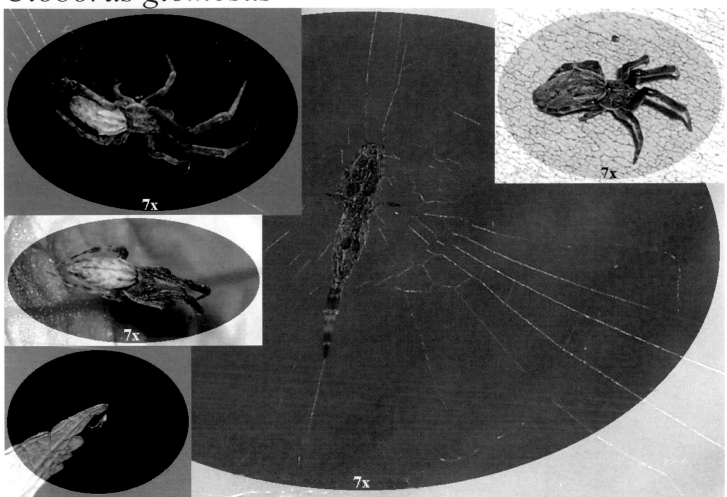

These very small spiders have no venom glands, and feathered hairs on their first tibiae. They spin small, broken-sectored orb webs {hackled band webs} on a slight slant, with a breeding web behind, and rest belly up and face down, resembling a small piece of chafe.

These delicate little spiders make their four to six inch webs in low bushes, dead branches, in hollow stumps, among rocks and between the staggered boards of fences around the yard. They are known from Florida, west to Texas, Nebraska and across much of southern Canada.

17x

17x

9.3x

The creature at the lower left is a male, who mated with the female along the top and right. The once perfect orb is left to become scraggly in cocooning season, since the female becomes more concerned with her upcoming brood than she is with catching food.

The females grow to a slight 2.8-4.5mm and the smaller males from 2.3-3.2mm. These spiders are from a separate evolutionary branch than other orb weavers, and make a 'V'-shaped stabilimenta to the hub.

8x

8.6x

Along the left is the impregnated female shown on previous pages, and is the same spider at the right and bottom, centre, generating her mass of eggs. She will guard them and then die in late summer, while the egg mass will separate into beaded globules and hatch in fall.

The nine species of *Uloborids* are unique in having no poison glands.

Large-jawed Orb Weavers
Tetragnathidae

Spotted Long-jawed Orb Weaver
Tetragnatha versicolor

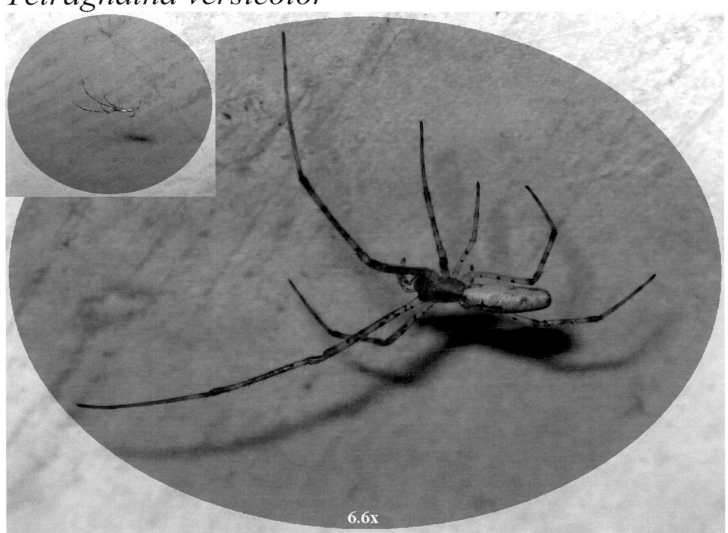

6.6x

Web weaving spiders have small eyes and rely on touch senses, almost oblivious of the surrounding world, and their senses radiate beyond their legs throughout the entire web. The species shown here has spotted legs, and smaller chelicerae than others in the family.

These spiders build radial orb webs in meadows, in bushes and long grass, usually near water, and are common throughout North America. The females are said to grow to about 6mm and the males to 5mm.

Lineate Long-jawed Orb Weaver
Tetragnatha laboriosa

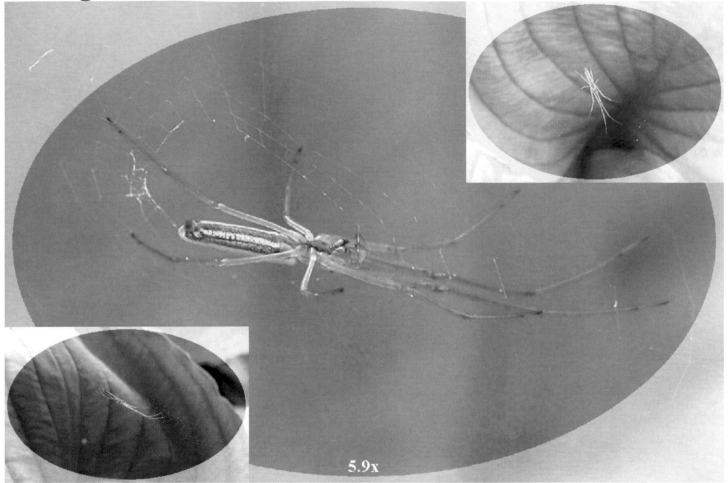

5.9x

The open hub in this spider's orb is obvious in the enlarged view above, and is typical to *Tetragnathids*. This species builds its orb slightly raised in elevation from the horizontal. Dwelling long distances from water, *T. laboriosa* are common in urban yards and gardens.

These are very common spiders that you may find both near and far from water, living in grasses, on plants and strewn between weeds and bushes, often in dry areas. They are known to inhabit the entire United States, yet they are also very common throughout southern Ontario.

The females typically grow to about 6mm and the males to 5mm, excluding the length of their chelicerae. They are usually dull yellow/brown to grey in general colour, with a brown longitudinal area on the abdomen, bordered by silvery stripes on either side.

Common to the genus, *T. laboriosa* build their orb webs with a hole

Lineate Long-jawed Orb Weaver

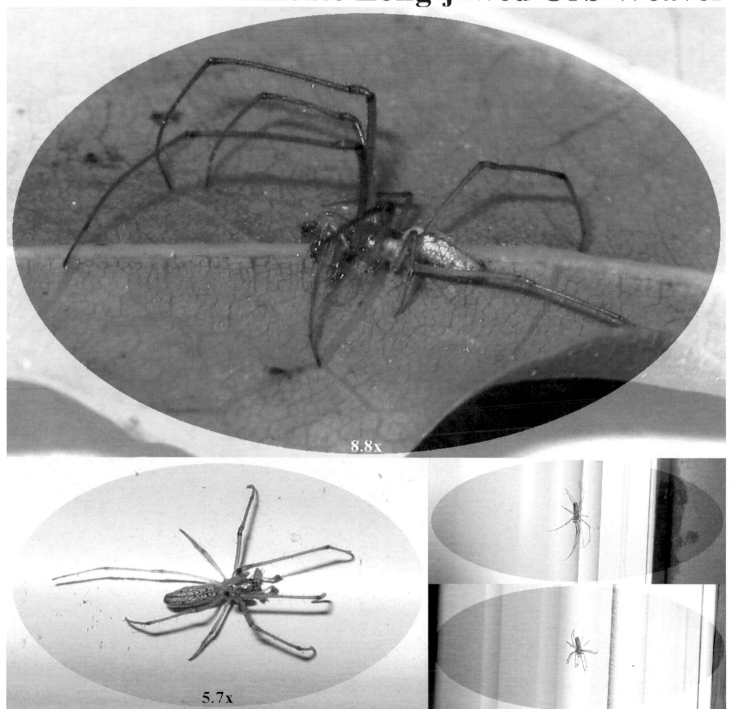

8.8x

5.7x

Notice the large clubbed endings at the tips of this males palps. Male spiders use these appendages as secondary genitals when mating with females. The lower left, enlarged photo shows the extended chelicerae, and the distinctive palps.

in the centre, where they rest upside and heads downward on a slightly elevated from horizontal web. Although the orb may only be about ten inches across, the bridge lines may span to two feet, or more.

Elongate Long-jawed Orb Weaver
Tetragnatha elongata

3.9x

Take special notice of the well developed chelicerae and sinuate fangs of these long bodied weavers. They have eight eyes, spaced in two parallel lines. The male above appears to have picked up a parasitic mite. Spiders of many kinds are often stricken by these pests.

These spiders build V-sectored radial webs in bushes and long grass in open meadows, and usually remain near water. The snare has an open hub where the spider sits face down. These large orb weavers are known throughout North America, but are most common in the east.

The females grow to about 9mm and males to 7.5mm, excluding their chelicerae, and their abdomens are quite long and swollen near

3x

3x

The folded fangs against the chelicerae are obvious in this beautifully marked female. The banks of open streams and rivers are a sure bet to find these distinctive and unforgettable orb weavers. The patterns are usually similar, yet they may be lighter or almost absent, and their bodies may be more silvery/grey or even brown, with the carapace always dark. Their menacing fangs are very effective against the larger insects found near shoresides.

the base in females, tapering toward the rear. They typically feed on midges, mosquitoes, crane flies, damselflies and a number of other weak flighted insects that mishap into their invisible webs.

The egg sacs are attached to twigs during late summer, and sparsely covered with a beadlike, greenish silk to secure them during the winter months. These are annual spiders that live for a mere one season.

Orb Weavers
Araneidae

Garden Spider
Araneus diadematus

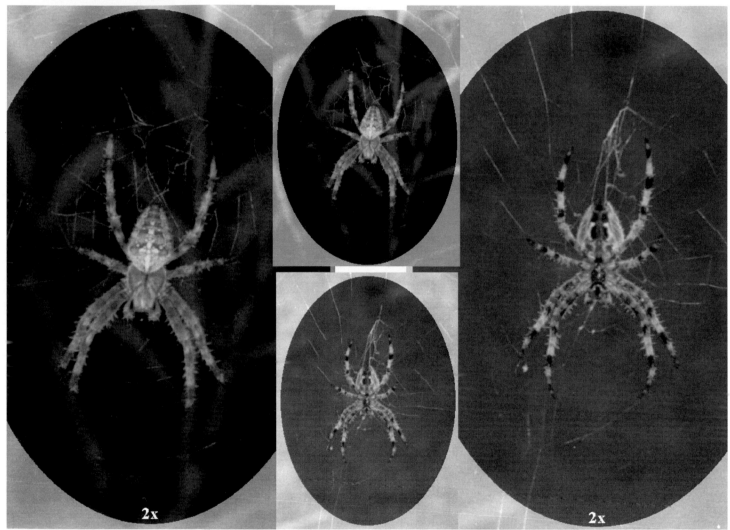

These well known spiders are easily recognised by the silver spots on the abdomen, forming a crucifix pattern. Above are the back view at top/centre and left, and the belly of a male at the bottom/centre and right. Several were strung between raspberry bushes.

These are very common spiders that spin their orb webs in city and suburban gardens, between our houses and shrubs. Introduced from Europe, they inhabit the Great Lakes, to Massachusetts and Boston.

Garden Spider

7.3x
9x
2.8x

Garden spiders come in a range of colours, from pale yellow to brown, or nearly black. They overwinter half grown, and mature after seven to eight moults by mid-summer.

The relatively large females grow from 11-18mm and the males from 5.5-11mm. They catch flying and jumping insects in their symetrical five or six sided orbs, which may be as much as twenty inches across.

Orb Weavers   **56**

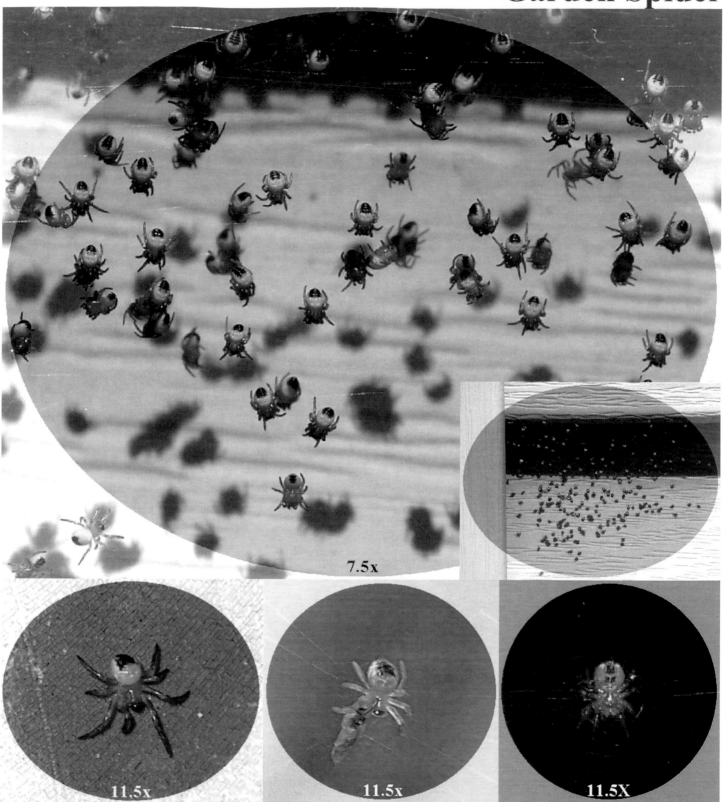

7.5x

11.5x　　　　11.5x　　　　11.5X

The cluster of spiderlings at top ballooned shortly after this shot was taken, and I found many of them strewn around my yard the next day - orbs constructed and all. Many spider strands that we brush from our faces are the result of these and other young spiders, attempting to float off in search of new horizons, effectively spreading their genes.

Furrow Spider
Araneus cornutus foliata

3.9x

Furrow spiders are very similar to the following *A. sericatus*, yet have shorter front legs, and a bright, usually entire folium on the back of their abdomens, with gold trim.

These spiders are common in moist, open clearings, and among the sages and reeds in marshlands from New England to Nebraska, ranging southward into Arizona, and east to North Carolina.

The females may be from 9-12mm and the males from 7-9mm.

Bridge Spider
Araneus sericatus

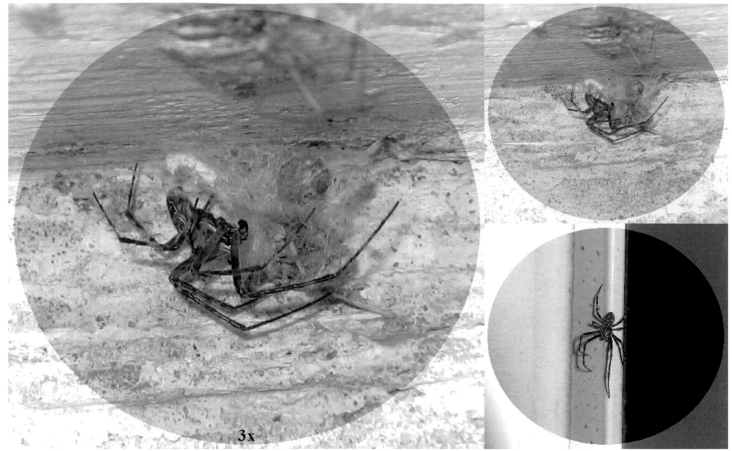

3x

You can see the silk shelter behind the male at left and top, right, situated in the corner below a bridge, above his web. These spiders wait at the end of the foundation line, sitting out on their webs only when the sun is weak. The male at lower right came home with me.

A. sericatus may be found amid tall grasses and shrubbery, but seem much more noticeable under bridges and culverts, etc. These are very common orb weavers from the Great Lakes east, and south to Virginia.

The females grow from 8-13mm and males from 5.5-8.5mm. They are much darker and more grey than the previous *A. cornutus*, and usually have broken edges around their dark brown to black folium.

They build spiralling orbs with non-sticky support lines and sticky vertical planes, making it easier to slide in on their prey of insects. They often sit at the centre of their webs with their heads facing down, or wait at their elevated resting site, connected by a signal line.

Bridge Spider

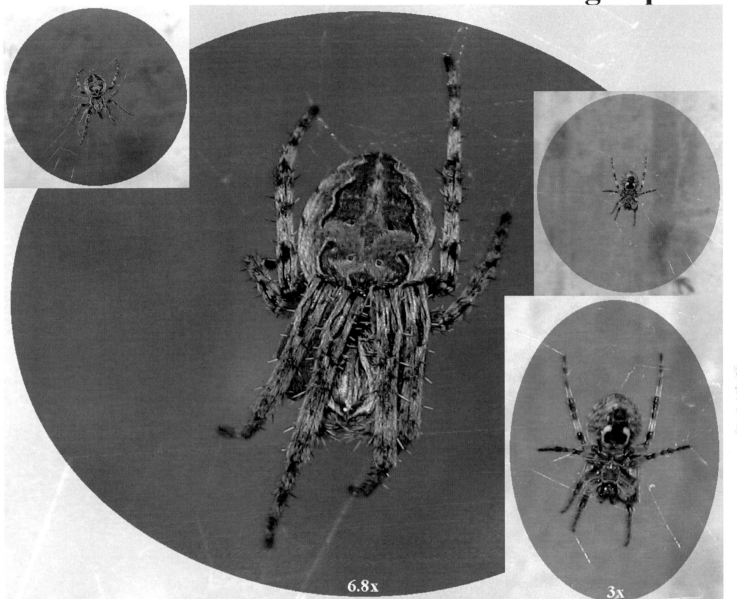

6.8x

3x

The underbelly, at the right, and the patterns of the dorsal folium are very distinctive in this species, as they are throughout the *Araneids* as a whole. The views above are those of a female that I found, yes, below a bridge. These are social spiders, building their orbs in close proximity with each other, sharing the bounty of damselflies, grasshoppers and such.

As with other orb weavers, these have very poor eyesight, even though they have eight small eyes. Relying on sensors from their web through their feet to detect prey, their silk is strong and flexible enough to subdue all but the strongest flying insects, and is functional both during the day and night, reducing their need of vision.

They attach their egg sacs to plants, or foliage near their retreat.

Marbled Orb Weaver
Araneus marmoreus

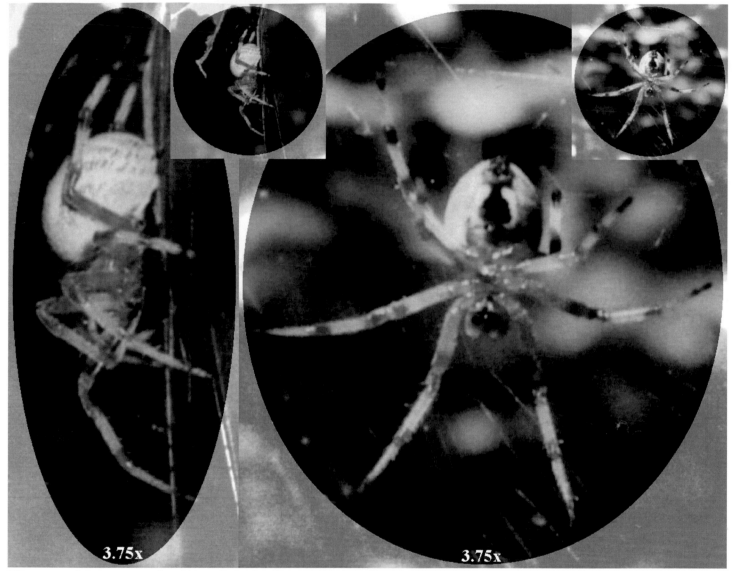

These spiders stay inside of their retreats during most of the day, to avoid becoming food themselves. A signal line connects the hub of the orb with the retreat, which is made with fastened leaves above the snare. They drop to the ground on a tether of silk if disturbed.

These beautiful weavers build their spiralling irregular orbs in wooded clearings and in tall grassy meadows, among trees and shrubs. They are common, although difficult to spot, throughout the eastern states to the northern Rockies and Alaska, south to Oregon and Texas.

The females range from 9-15mm and the males from 6-9mm. They usually rest in their retreat made of silk swathed leaves, or under bark

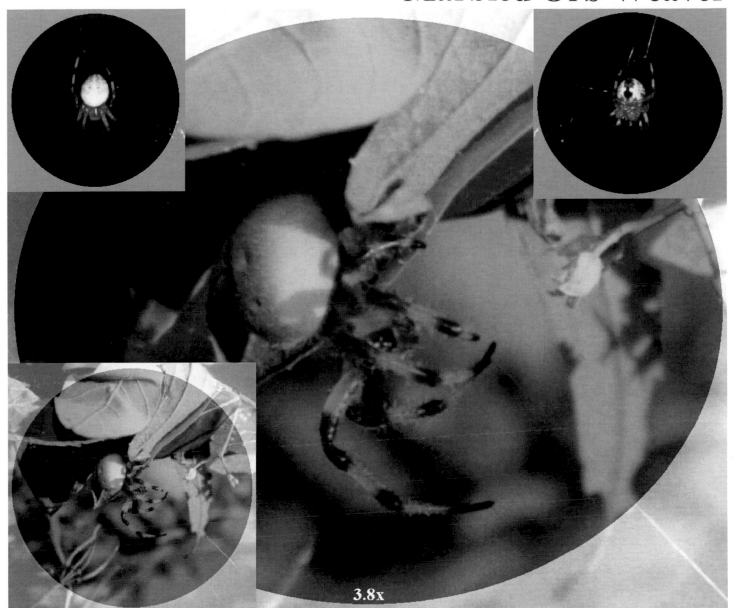

3.8x

When you spot an orb web, follow the main frame line until you notice healthy leaves carefully stitched together, opened facing slightly down and toward the web. By looking up inside you will see the spider resting in wait of an insect to flounder into its web.

if against a suitable tree. They connect a signal line from their retreat to the hub of their web to detect the motions of a trapped insect, and quickly slide down to greet it using their curved, web-sliding claws.

Their orange eggs are laid in flattened, cocoon like egg sacs, made of loose white silk, and are attached to a leaf near their retreats in early autumn. These weavers may overwinter as either eggs or spiderlings.

Shamrock
Araneus trifolium

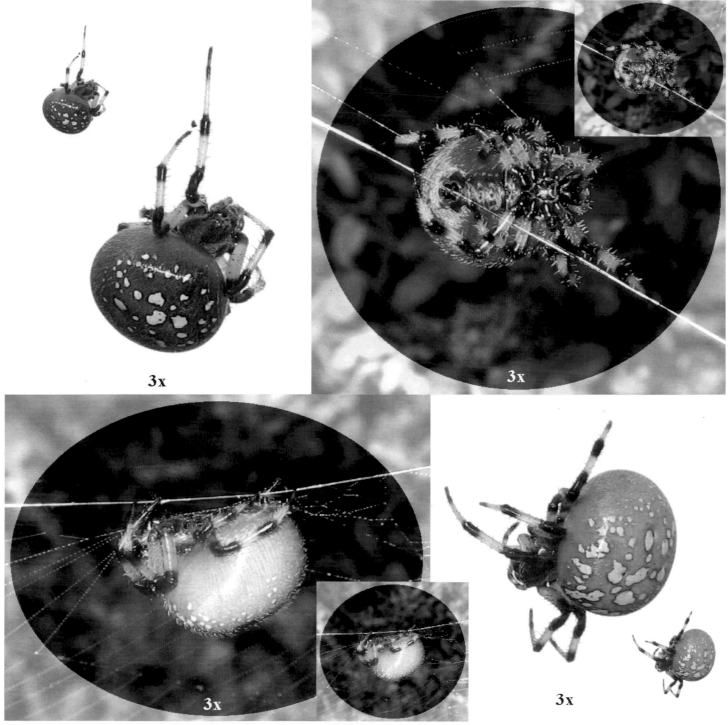

3x

3x

3x

3x

Resembling white-spotted candy, these spiders remain hidden inside their retreats during the day, tending their webs when required. Shamrocks rebuild their orbs each night.

Shamrocks prefer the open, grassy areas of meadows and pastures around woodland edges in the United States and adjacent Canada.

Ranging greatly in colours, *A. trifolium* always bear white spots on their abdomens.

Female Shamrocks grow from 9-18mm and males from 4.5-5.5mm. Their retreat and web are similar with the previous *A. marmoreus*.

Spotted Sun Spider
Araniella displicata

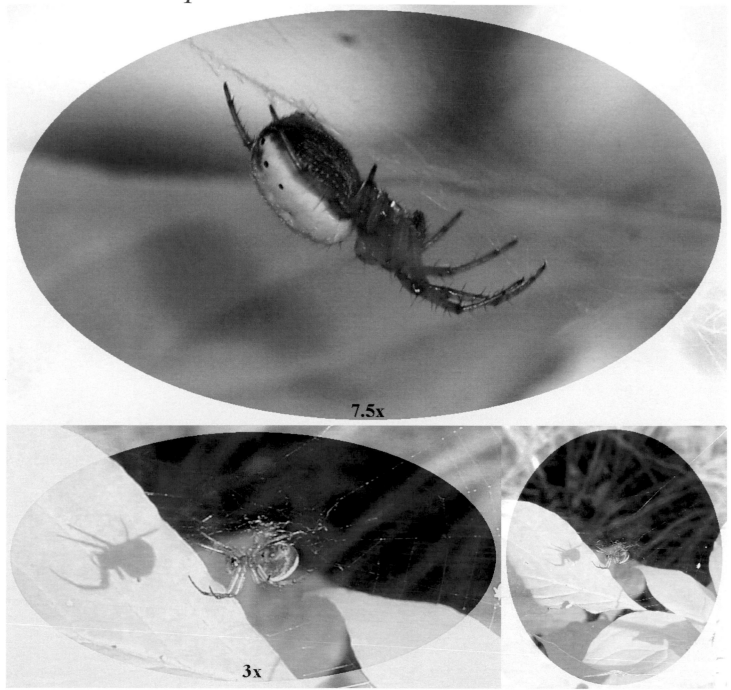

7.5x

3x

The abdomens of *A. displicata* may be white, yellow or pink, with 3 pairs of black spots on the posterior half. Their webs are slightly elevated, and the spider rests upside down.

These bright and scarcely noticed orb weavers build their webs in tall grass and shrubs throughout the United States and southern Canada. The females range in size from 4-8mm and the males from 4-6mm.

Branch-tip Spider
Eustala anastera

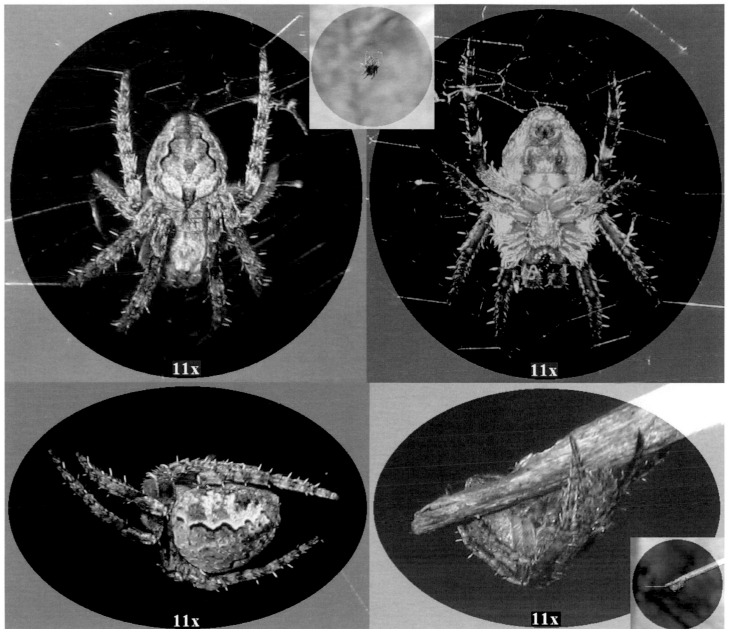

11x · 11x · 11x · 11x

If you've ever strayed from the trail in a forest, you've brushed away webs strung from tree branch to tree branch made by these interesting little jewels. Their abdomens display a considerable variety in patterns, and may be lime, brown, red or grey in colour tincture.

E. anastera are very common in the low branches of trees, shrubs and bushes where there is broken sunlight. They are well known from New England, south to Florida and west to the Rocky Mountains.

The females grow from 5.4-9mm and the males from 4-6mm.

Neoscona Orb Weaver
Neoscona arabesca

The spider shown here was found in the spring, and had overwintered as a preadolescent. Although the spider will grow larger than the life-size images above at top left and bottom centre, they are still relatively small weavers. Small or not, these spiders are notably venomous, and are capable of biting if mishandled - like most of our local orb weavers.

These beautifully marked weavers build their webs in tall grass and between low bushes, typically remaining close to the ground. You may find them along trail sides in open woods, near the shorelines of marshes, and in meadows throughout most of North America.

The females grow from 5-8mm and the males from 5-6mm. Females lack the yellow markings prominent in males (above). Their webs may be 40cm across, and the spider rests at the hub, building no retreat.

Neat Orb Weaver
Mangora acalypha

With only slight resemblance to the preceding *N. arabesca*, these weavers are known in Europe, N. Africa and much of Asia - only recently brought here, most likely with plants. Their finely meshed, dense orbs are rebuilt each morning, and consumed again at night.

These small orb weavers sit in their webs near woodland edges and in gardens among shrubs and rank weeds, usually seen between June and September. The females grow to 6mm, and the males to 4mm.

Star-bellied Spider
Acanthepeira stellata

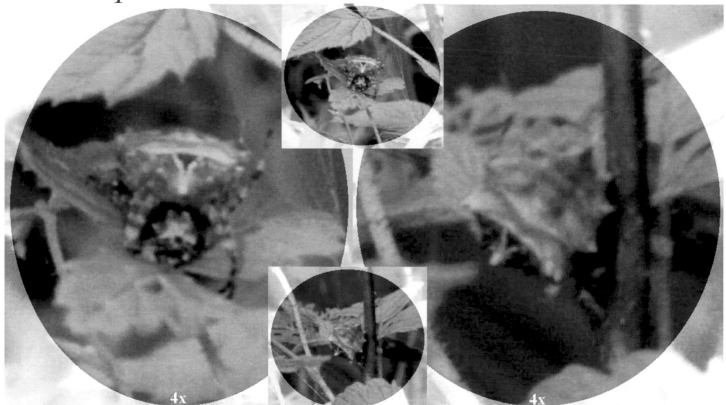

Unfortunately, these pictures are not the best in blow-up quality, yet this spider could not be left out of this book. Although I didn't see the underside of this creature, the name is in obvious reference to the ventral belly markings. This spider seems to fit in well amid the raspberry bushes she was on, yet I couldn't find evidence of either her web or shelter.

Star-bellied spiders typically prefer areas with tall grass, wildflowers, shrubs and low bushes to set up their orbs and retreats. Of the three similar species in our area at large, *A. stellata* are common, but not abundant (depending on your local environment) throughout New England and Minnesota, and range south into Texas and Florida.

The females grow to a medium 11-12mm and the smaller males from 6-7mm. Although most orb weavers (and *Araneids* as a whole) have soft abdomens, this species has a hardened body, accompanied by rigid, cone-like protuberances - reminding one of a prickly berry. This tough exterior may well make them much less palatable, and perhaps even less appealing to a greater number of would-be predators.

3.7x

3.7x

Spiders all have the same parts, yet each species has a uniqueness to each part. This spiny little male seemed quite content, and totally oblivious to my presence as he busily constructed the framework between stalks of wild grass to spin out his orb-shaped snare. These spiders feed on a variety of insects, including small grasshoppers and damselflies.

Cone-tailed Weaver
Cyclosa conica

9x

I found this female at the side of a trail with her twelve inch wide orb situated between the dead branches of a fallen tree, and thriving springtime weeds. The kaki string of debris is more easily spotted than the spiders themselves, because they deliberately attach each meal to their stabilimentum with silk, thus camouflaging themselves to appear as nothing more than another dead insect in the string. *C. conica* strongly resemble *Conopistha rufa** in the Comb-footed family, which have an exceptionally long horn on their tails.

These are very cold tolerant creatures that are active from the earliest warm days of spring, until the frostiest days of fall, and you are very likely to encounter their snares built low to the ground in open woods. They are both common and very abundant throughout North America.

Mature females are typically between 5.3-7.5mm and males from 3.6-4mm. Their colours are variable from grey to black, with hues of tan to red, and their caudal hump becomes more prominent with age, which is less pronounced in males. These weavers usually provide their orb with a short stabilimentum above and below the hub, lining it with old insect meal remains. They overwinter and mature in spring.

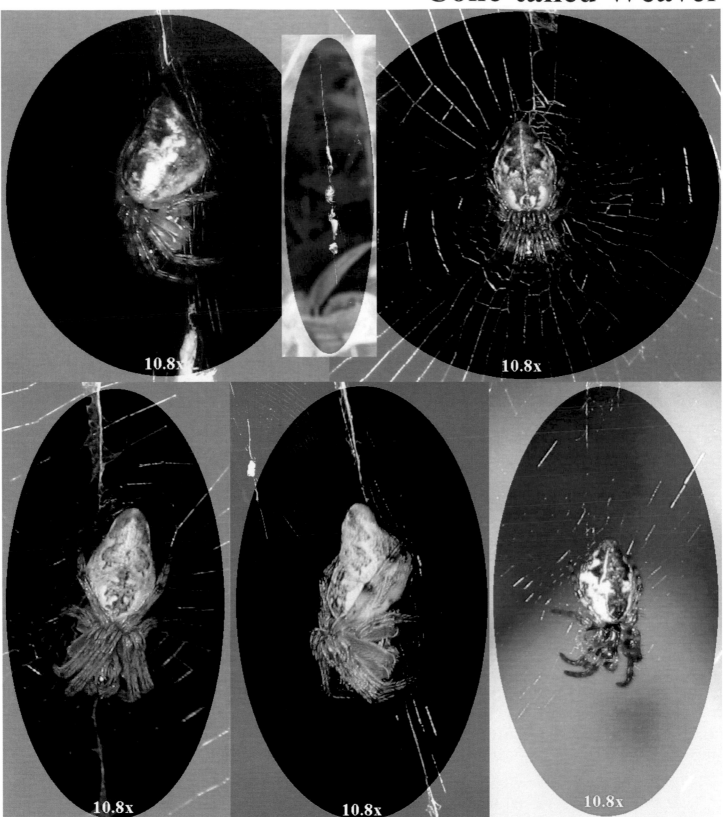

10.8x

10.8x

10.8x

10.8x

10.8x

The enlarged views at lower left and centre are of an adolescent female found in the fall. The top views are those of a young male, as is the lower right. Once mating has taken place in spring, the female adds her egg sac to the relative safety of the debris string.

Banded Argiope
Argiope trifasciata

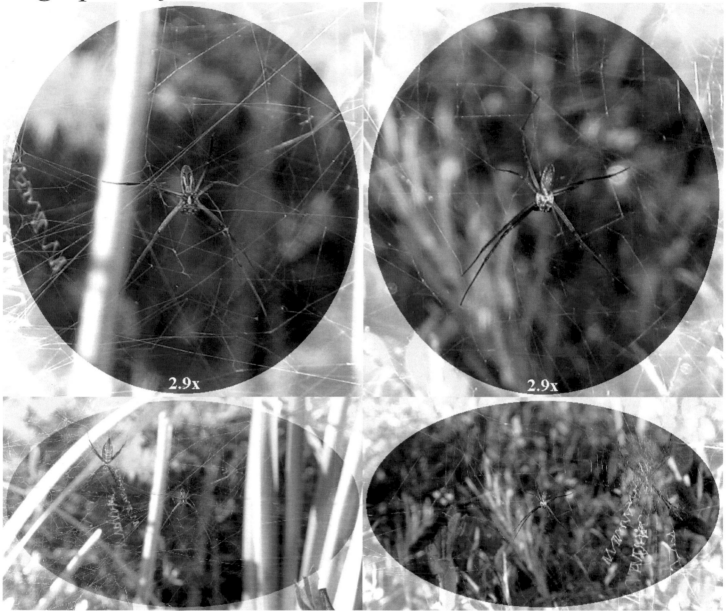

The left and right are complimentary ventral and dorsal views of a male, which has constructed a tiny imperfect snare facing the female's web, which is visible in the back and foreground (no focus-NS) of the lower, life-size views, showing three zig-zagged stabilimentum, which are often left out altogether. These spiders sit facing down at the hub of their snares in wait of grasshoppers to strike their webs, and build no retreat.

A. trifasciata live in open sunny places among shrubs and tall grass near bogs and marshes, yet also abound in drier meadows throughout North America, and range both the temperate and subtropical world.

4.9x

3.6x

Females in this species can grow to a hefty 25mm, dwarfing the tiny males at a mere 5.5mm. An empregnated female is preparing a grasshopper meal at left/centre, while all other views are of an unmated female. Their tough papery covered egg sacs overwinter.

Black-and-yellow Argiope
Argiope aurantia

A dorsal view showing the spider's back is shown at left, and the ventor showing the finely meshed hub, between the stabilimentum is clearly visible on the right. It is said that males build their web in outlying areas of a female's web, or at least very close at hand. Like other *Argiopes*, *A. aurantia* prefer sunny, calm, open areas, where insect prey is bountiful.

These boldly displayed weavers build their distinctive orbs among shrubbery, tall plants and wildflowers in meadows and home gardens, yet prefer moist wooded areas near stream banks and marshes. These spiders are readily recognised throughout most of the United States and southern Canada, being scarce in the Rockies and the Great Basin.

The females grow to a hefty size of 19-28mm and males range from 5-8mm. They build spiraling vertical orbs, which radiate from the centre with a conspicuous, vertical zig-zag. The spiders sit facing down in the hub of the stabilimentum at the centre of their snare, and no retreat is made. They feed on small flying and jumping insects, and will vigorously vibrate their web becoming an indistinct blur, or will drop to the ground using a dragline and hide if they feel threatened.

The female attaches a spherical egg sac close to her resting position in the late summer, and soon dies. The eggs hatch later in autumn, with

As long as you don't disturb the plants shoring their webs, the poor vision of orb weavers renders them oblivious to someone watching their activities. A typical egg sac is shown secured to bullrushes in the upper right, a female wrapping a rubyspot damselfly with silk at bottom left, and the other views show females with both yellow and orange femur.

the first instar spiderlings overwintering in the sac. The large egg-sacs (20-25mm) are conspicuous, tough, pear-shaped, papery covered spheroids made with several layers of different kinds of silk, and may take several hours to construct. They are usually strung and well secured in plants nearby their orbs in the fall or in early spring.

Experiments have shown that the stabilimentum wards birds from flying through their webs, and I'd imagine deer steering clear as well.

Glossary

arachnophobia; a fear of the class of air-breathing arthropods, known as *Arachnida*, including scorpions, mites, etc.

ballooning; the flight of spiders by spinning of silken strands.

carapace; hard upper covering combining head and thorax of *Arachnids*.

chelicerae; first pair of two-segmented appendages in spiders with distal portions being the fangs used to inject venom into their prey.

epigynum; epigyne; apparatus for storing male spermatozoa, immediately in front of opening in female reproductive organs.

fang; secondary portion of chelicerae used to inject venom.

folium; looping patterns on upper abdomen in spiders.

gossamer; fine strands of silk left by spiders after ballooning.

hackled band; composite threads made by cribellate spiders.

heart patch; coloured marking stemming from the foreward portion of a spiders abdomen tapering by about mid-way, covering the heart.

necrosis; death or decay of tissue in a particular part of the body.

New England; six NE states including Me., Ve., N.H., Mass., R.I., & Conn. For the purposes of this book it includes Southern Ontario.

palpus; segmented appendage of pedipalp bearing reproductive organs in males; small in females.

pedipalp; second pair of appendages on head of spiders used in crushing prey and bearing distal palpus.

pheromones; chemical substance emitted by and detectable by male and female spiders, especially during courtship and mating.

scopula; small, dense tuft or extensive brush of hairs or setae.

spinneret; one of several fingerlike abdominal appendages of spiders used in spinning silk.

stabilimentum; special band of silk across centre of web in some spiders.

venom; poison secreted by some snakes, spiders, insects, etc., introduced into the body by a bite or sting.

Bibliography

- National Audubon Society; **Field Guide to North American Insects and Spiders**' Borzoi, 1980, 1985, Random House Canada.

- Friends of Algonquin Park; **Insects of Algonquin Provincial Park**'
   Steve Marshall, 1997, HLR Publishing Group, Arnprior, ON.

- Collins Gem; **Spiders - From the Deadliest to the Biggest on Earth**'; Paul Hillyard (text), 1997, 2004, HarperCollinsPublisher, Bishopbriggs, Glasgow. Printed in Italy by Amadeus.

- A Golden Guide; **Spiders and their Kin**'
   St Martin's Press; Herbert W Levi & Lorna R Levi, 2002
   175 Fifth Ave, New York, NY, 10010.

- Pictured Key Nature Series; **How To Know The Spiders**', 2nd Edition; H E Jaques, 1rst Edition, 1953; B J Kaston, San Diego State College, 1972, Wm C Brown Co. Publishers, Dubuque, Iowa USA.

- American Museum of Natural History; **American Spiders**', 2nd Edition; Willis J Gertsch, Ph.D., 1979, Litton Educational Publishing, Inc since 1949. Published by Van Nostrand Reinhold Company, 135 W 50th St, New York, NY, 10020 USA.

- Blandford; **Spiders of the World**'; Rod & Ken Preston-Mafham, 1984+1993. Distributed by Stirling Publishing Co., Inc., 387 Park Ave.S, New York, NY, 10016-8810 USA.

- Lutterworth Press; **Insects and other Invertebrates In Colour**' Adapted/Revised from Swedish Edition, 1973 by Ron M Dobson, 1975. Interbook Publishing AB Sweden.

- Lone Pine Field Guide; **Bugs of Alberta**'; John H Acorn, 2000. Lone Pine Publishing, 10145 - 81 Ave, Edmonton AB, Canada.

Index

(*) mentioned but not described

This book of **Spiders** is my fifth, preceded by my books of **Amphibians & Reptiles**, **Butterflies**, **Mushrooms I**, and **Damselflies & Dragonflies**.

With so much flora and fauna to describe, future books in the *'Life-size'* series will include further categories such as; **Mushrooms II**, various **Insects**, **Wildflowers**, **Trees & Shrubs** and possibly others - all pertaining to *'Southern Ontario'*.

Look for these books coming soon.